# MAKO SHARKS

Anne Welsbacher

## Capstone Press

MINNEAPOLIS

Printed in the United States of America.

Capstone Press • 2440 Fernbrook Lane • Minneapolis, MN 55447

Editorial Director    John Coughlan
Managing Editor    John Martin
Production Editor    James Stapleton
Copy Editor    Thomas Streissguth

**Library of Congress Cataloging-in-Publication Data**

Welsbacher, Anne, 1955-
    Mako sharks / by Anne Welsbacher.
      p.  cm. -- (Sharks)
    Includes bibliographical references (p.  ) and index.
    ISBN  1-56065-272-1
    1. Shortfin mako--Juvenile literature. 2. Mako sharks--
Juvenile literature. [1. Mako sharks. 2. Sharks.] I. Title. II.
Series: Welsbacher, Anne, 1955-  Sharks.
    QL638.95.L3W44  1996
    597'.31--dc20                                      95-7351
                                                       CIP
                                                       AC
 99  98  97  96  95        6  5  4  3  2  1

# Table of Contents

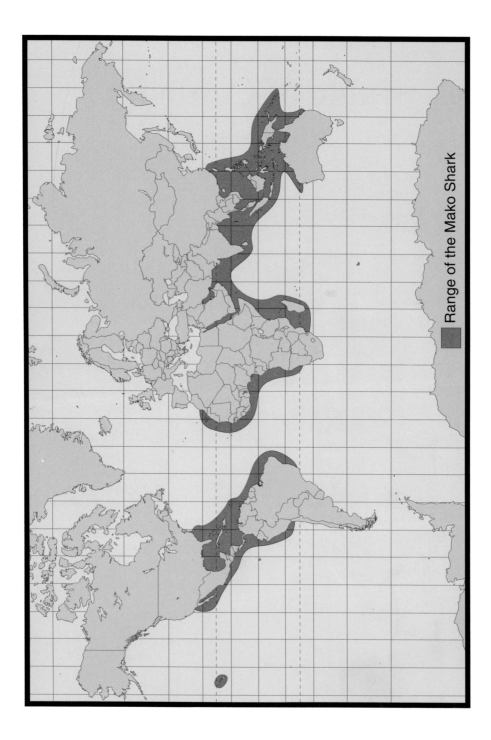

Range of the Mako Shark

# Facts about Mako Sharks

*Scientific name:* Isurus oxyrinchus

*Common names:* Mako, shortfin mako, sharp-nosed mackerel shark. In Australia, it's called the blue pointer.

*Closest relatives:* Longfin mako, great white shark, and porbeagle.

*Description:* A streamlined shark with sharply pointed snout, dark eyes, slender body, large teeth, and small back fin.

*Length:* Makos reach 12 feet (3.6 meters). Average length is about 6.5 feet (2 meters).

*Weight:* Makos weigh up to 1,000 pounds (453 kilograms); the largest weigh as much as 1,300-plus pounds (591 kilograms).

*Color:* Dark metallic blue above and white below.

*Food:* Fish and squid.

*Location:* Makos swim in the warm and temperate (nearly warm) oceans of the world.

# Chapter 1

# Built for Speed

It's a furious fighter. It will jump high into the air. It will jump right into a boat. It will even attack a boat.

It's built to move fast. It has been clocked at 60 miles (97 kilometers) an hour.

It has teeth like daggers, teeth that can tear apart the biggest prey.

It's the mako, the fastest, meanest-looking shark in the world.

## Fast in the Water

Makos are built like good airplanes. They are **streamlined** so the water does not drag on

**Isurus oxyrinchus** glides near the surface, looking for prey.

them. They have cone-shaped snouts that come to a sharp point. The snout cuts easily through the water. Their powerful tails give them a lot of thrust, like a jet engine.

A mako moves fast when it is chasing prey or trying to break free from a fishing hook.

Makos have been clocked at 60 miles (97 kilometers) per hour. But their usual chasing speed is about 20 to 35 miles (32 to 56 kilometers) or more per hour.

When the mako is not chasing food or in danger, it cruises at a slow 2 miles (3.2 kilometers) per hour. Most sharks swim less than a mile, or about 1.6 kilometers, an hour.

At that pace, makos can keep on swimming for a long time. One mako traveled 36 miles (58 kilometers) a day for 37 days. Another shark swam 1,700 miles (2,700 kilometers) from Virginia in the United States to the West Indies.

## Big Blue

Although most makos are about the size of a large human being, makos that live a long time may reach about 10 to 12 feet (3 to 3.7 meters) in length.

Teeth of fossil makos have been found. They show that ancient makos may have weighed two tons and may have measured 20 feet long.

Like many sharks, makos are dark on top and light on the bottom. Their bright metallic-blue backs darken to dark blue when they are out of the water. A band of silver divides the blue from the white underside. A mako's shiny skin is smooth.

The mako and its relatives can be quickly recognized by their tails. Unlike most sharks, their tails are curved, with the parts above and below the body about equal in size and shape. In fact, the mako family's scientific name, *Isuridae,* means "equal tails."

Many sharks have two **dorsal**, or back, fins. The mako has one fairly large one in the middle of the body and a much smaller one back toward the tail.

## A Keel for Speed

The mako's streamlined body helps it move fast. Another thing that helps is its **keel**. The keel is a hard, flat part that sticks out from the narrow body just before the tail.